Copyright © 2015 Ocean Coloring

All Rights Reserved Worldwide

Ocean Coloring Book

PSYCHEDELIC STRESS-RELIEVING FISH

A Coloring Book For Adults

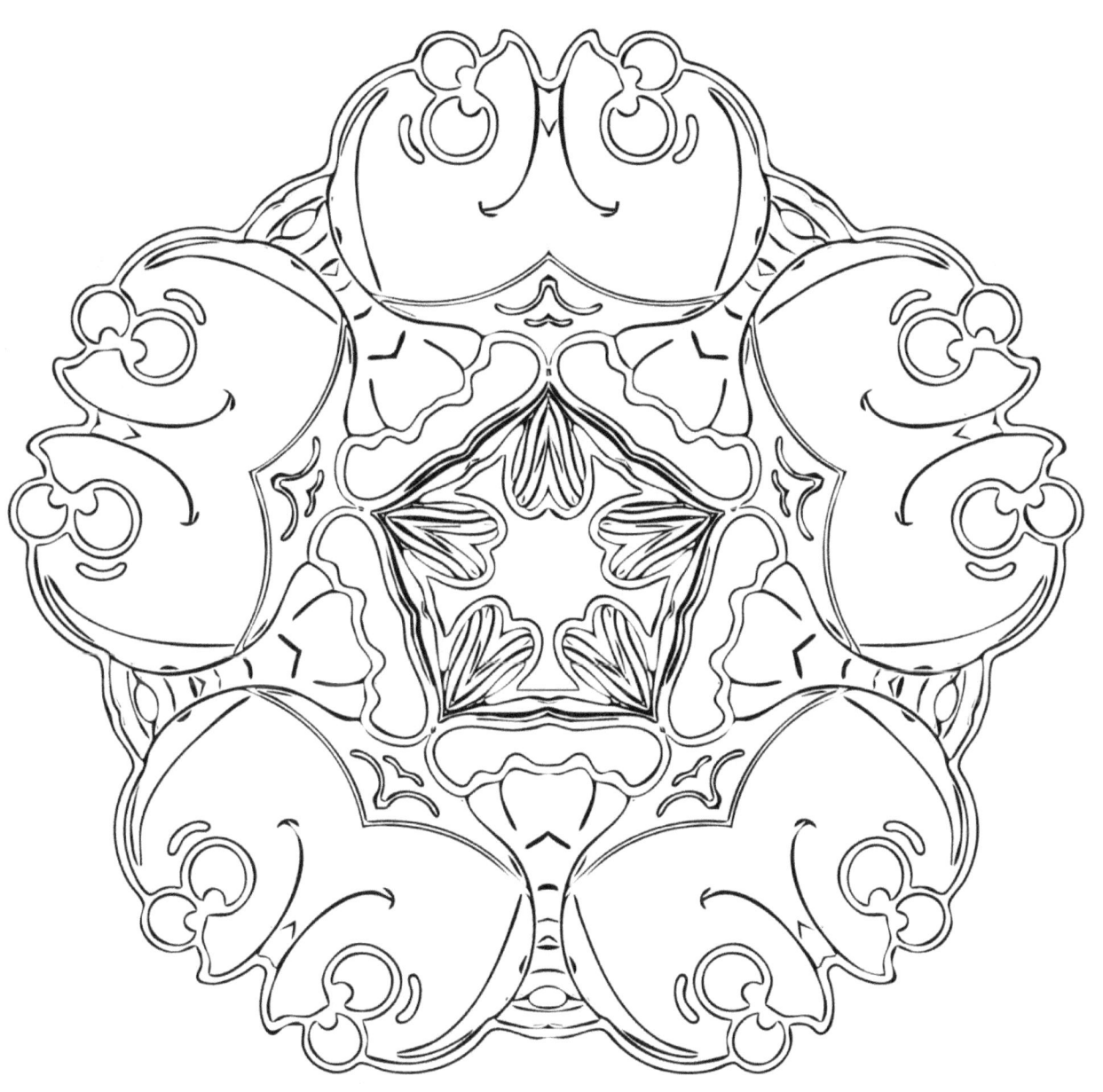

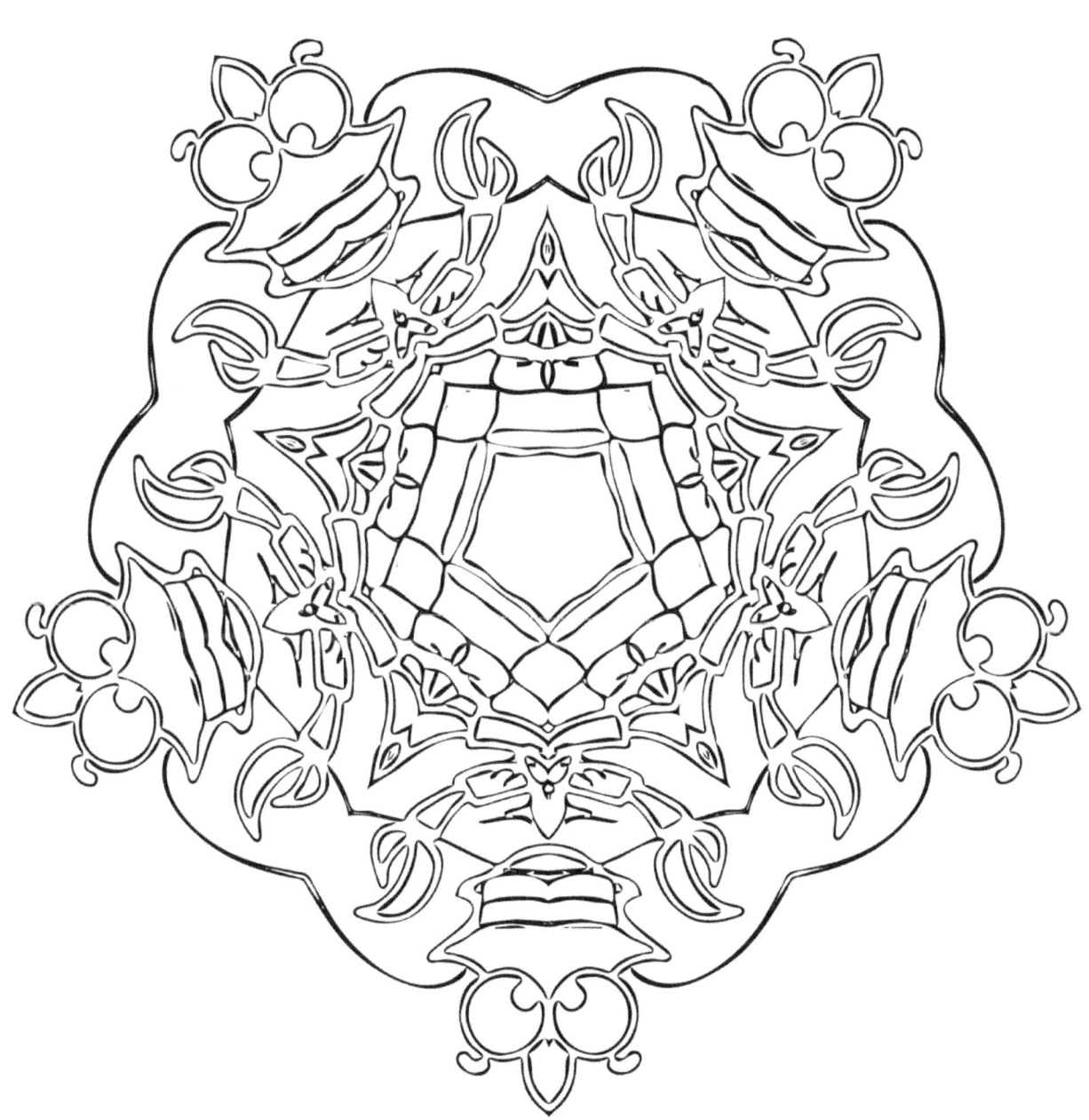

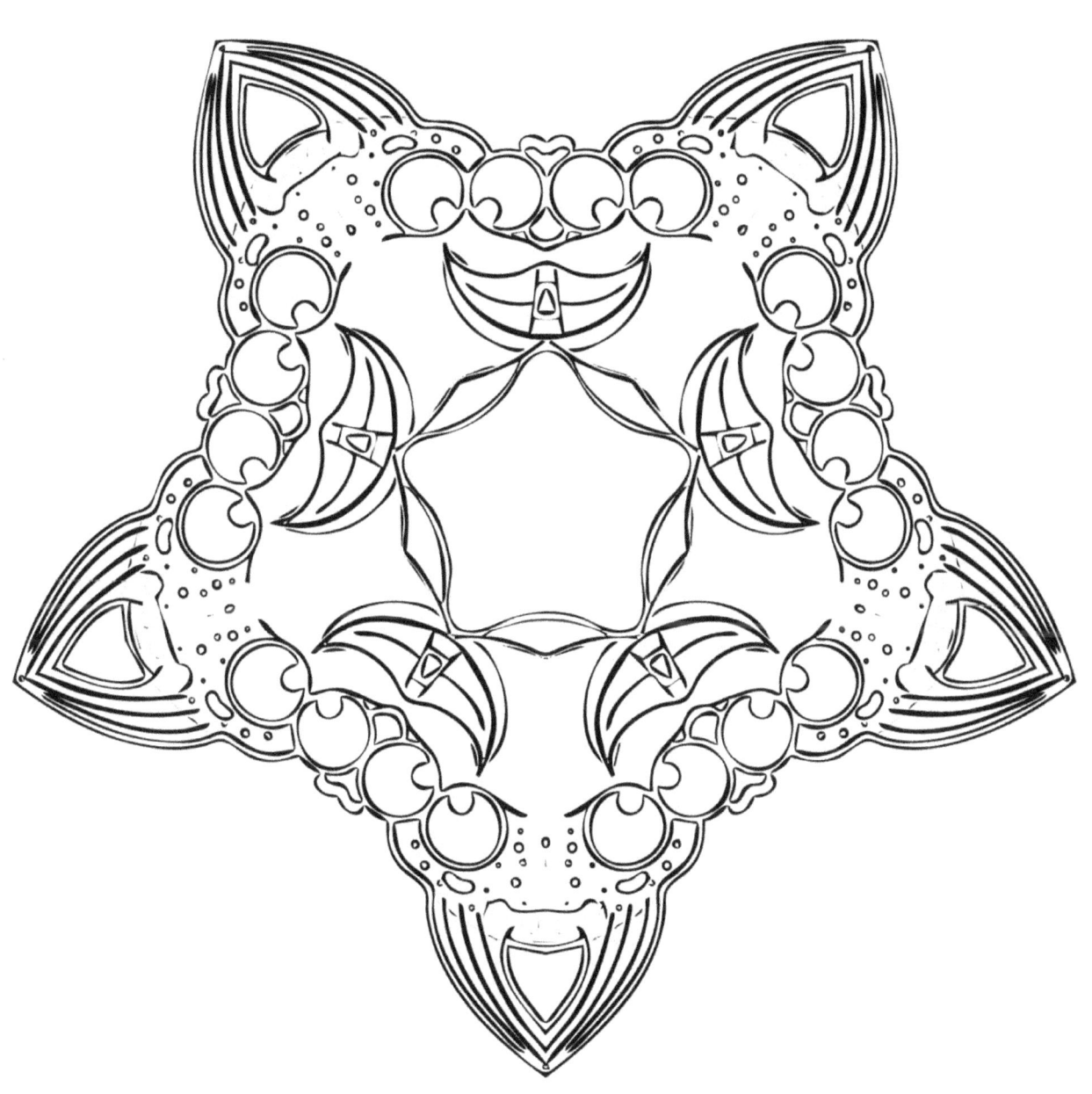

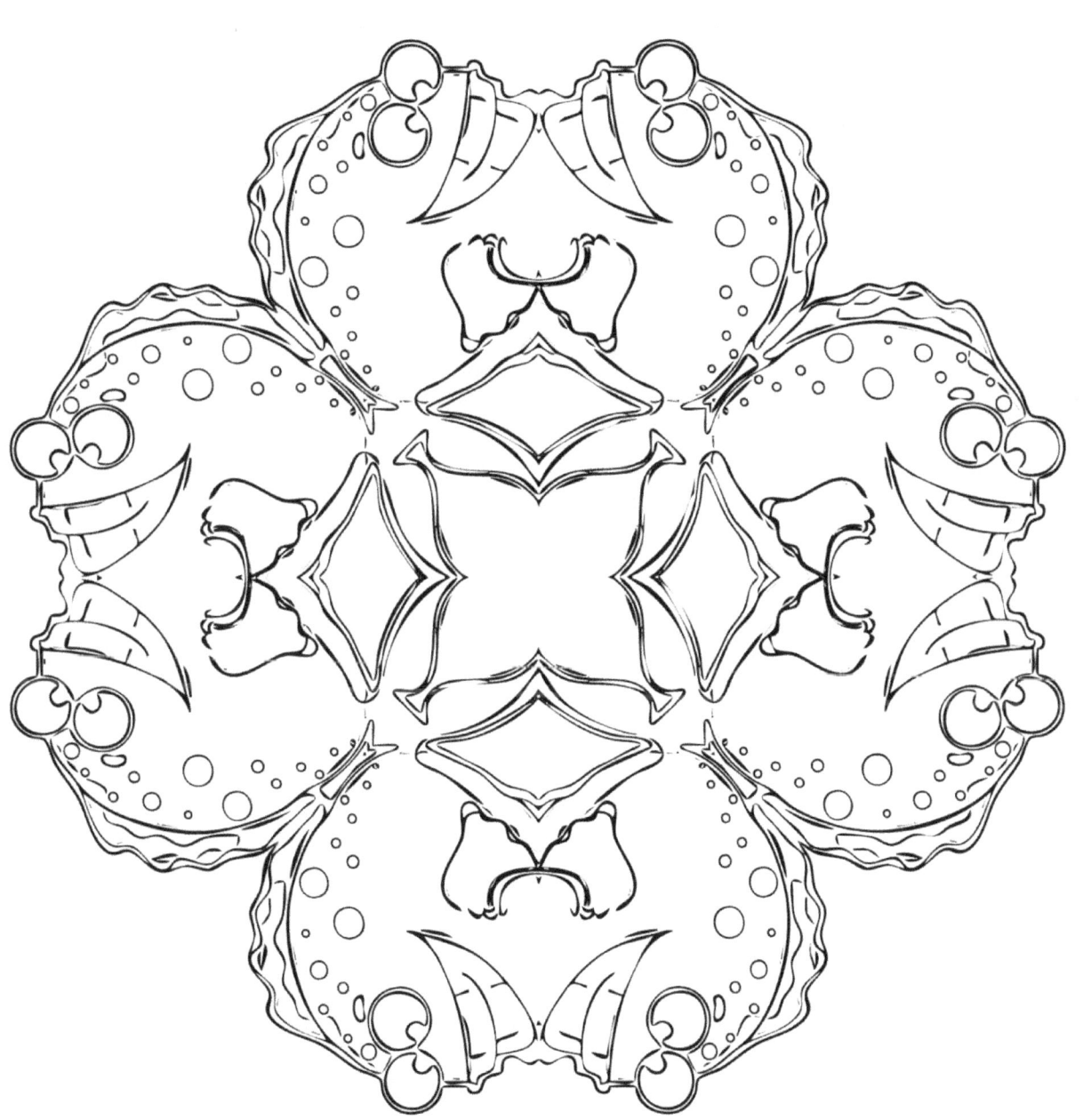

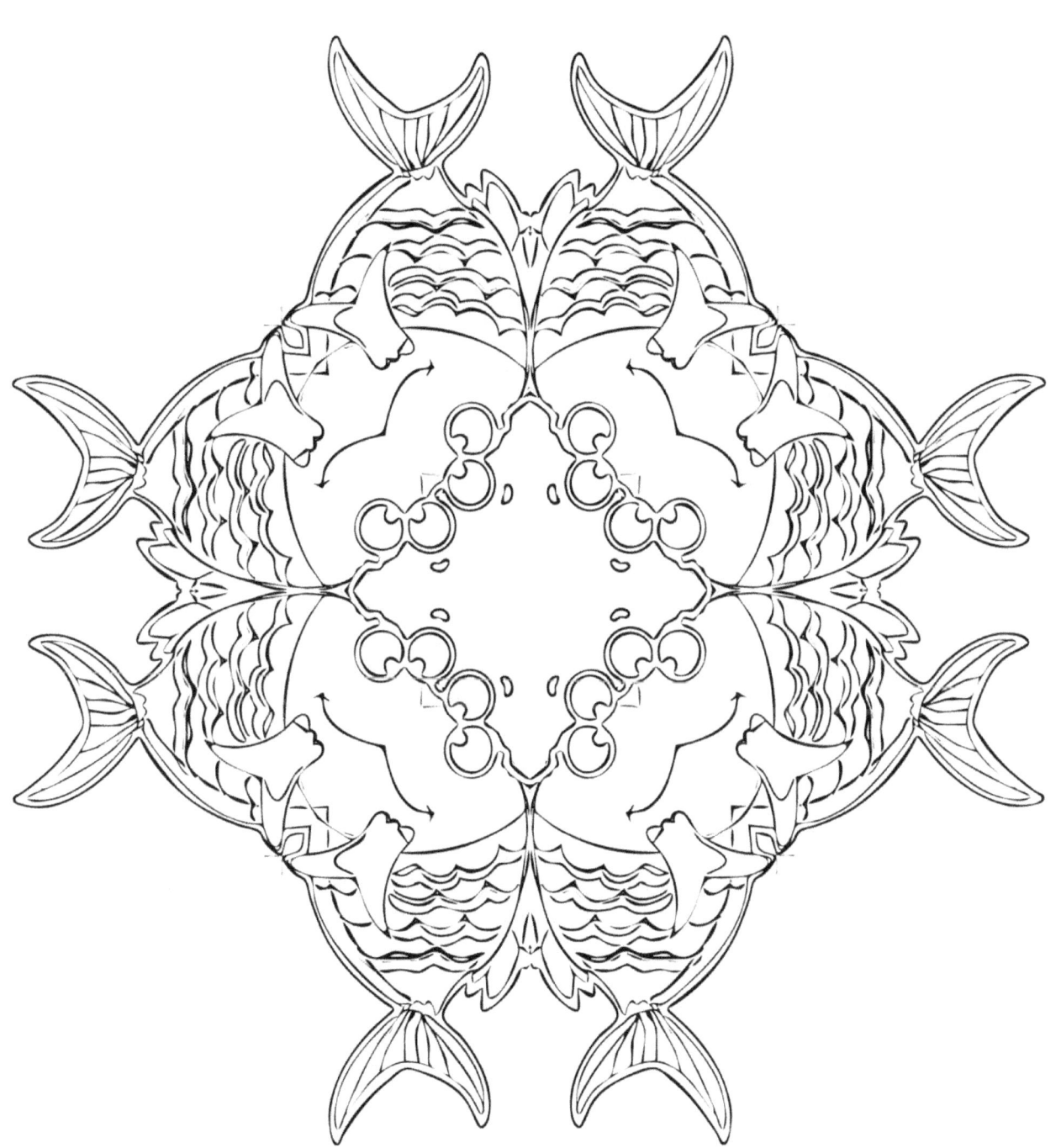

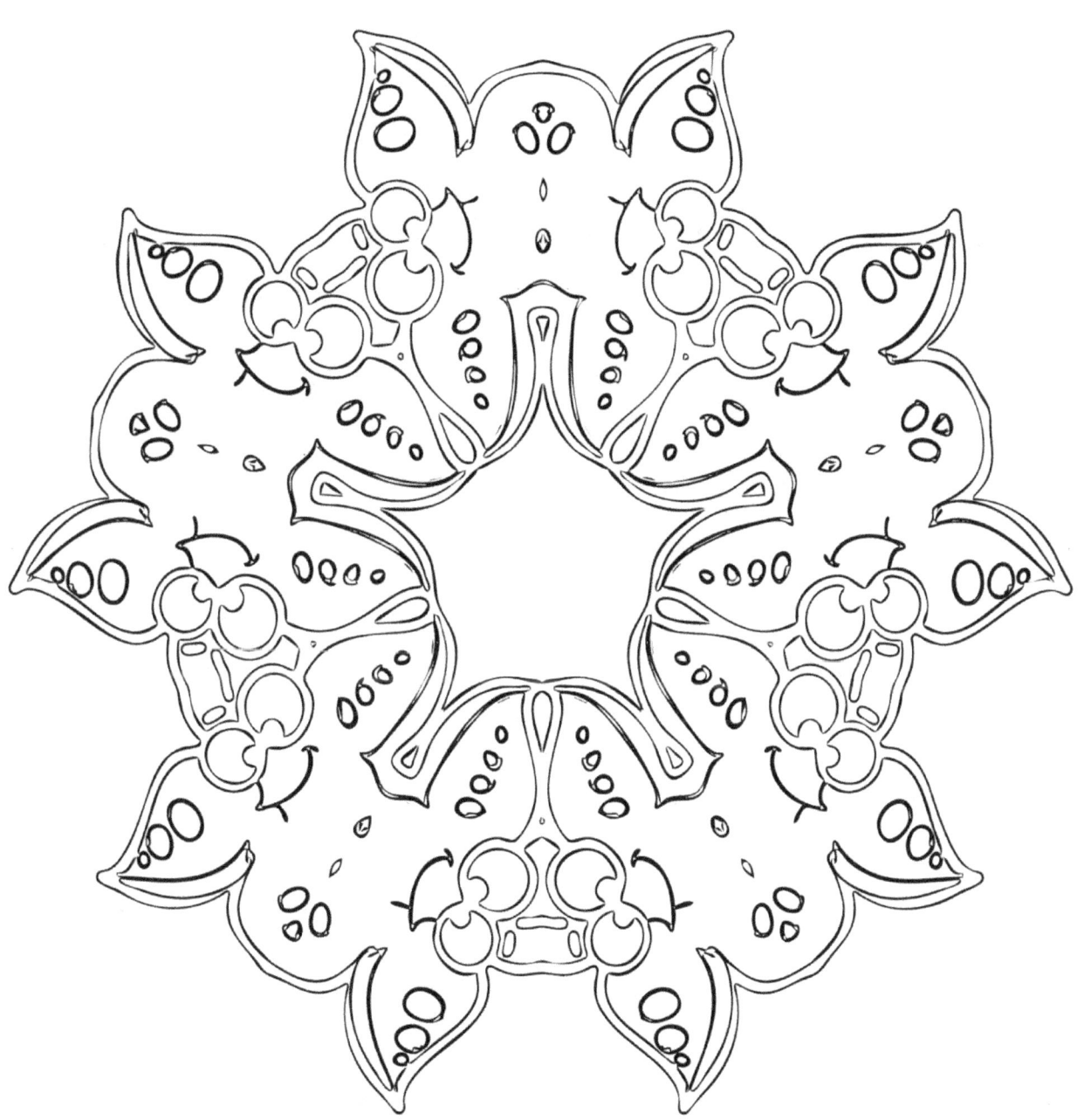

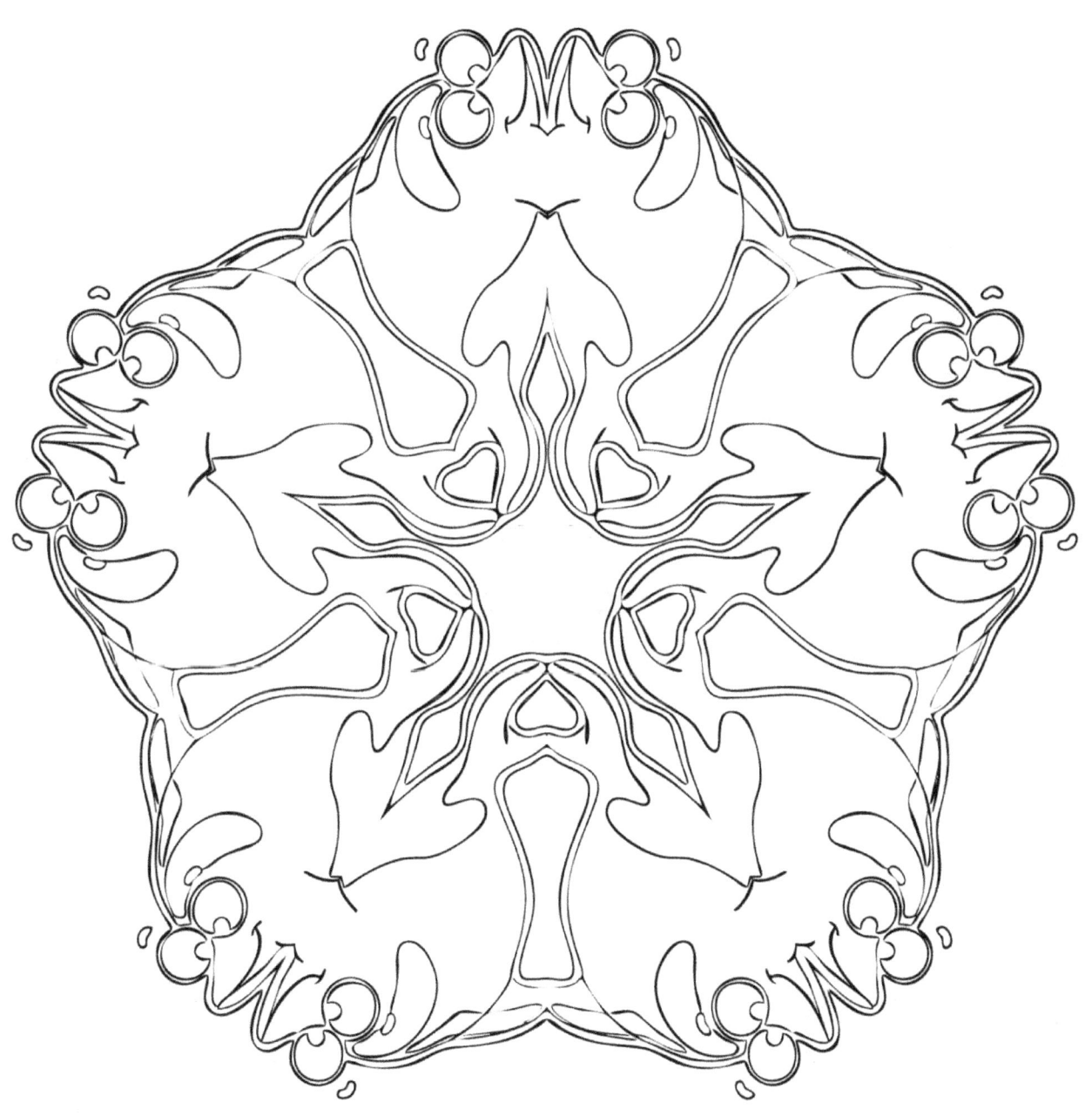

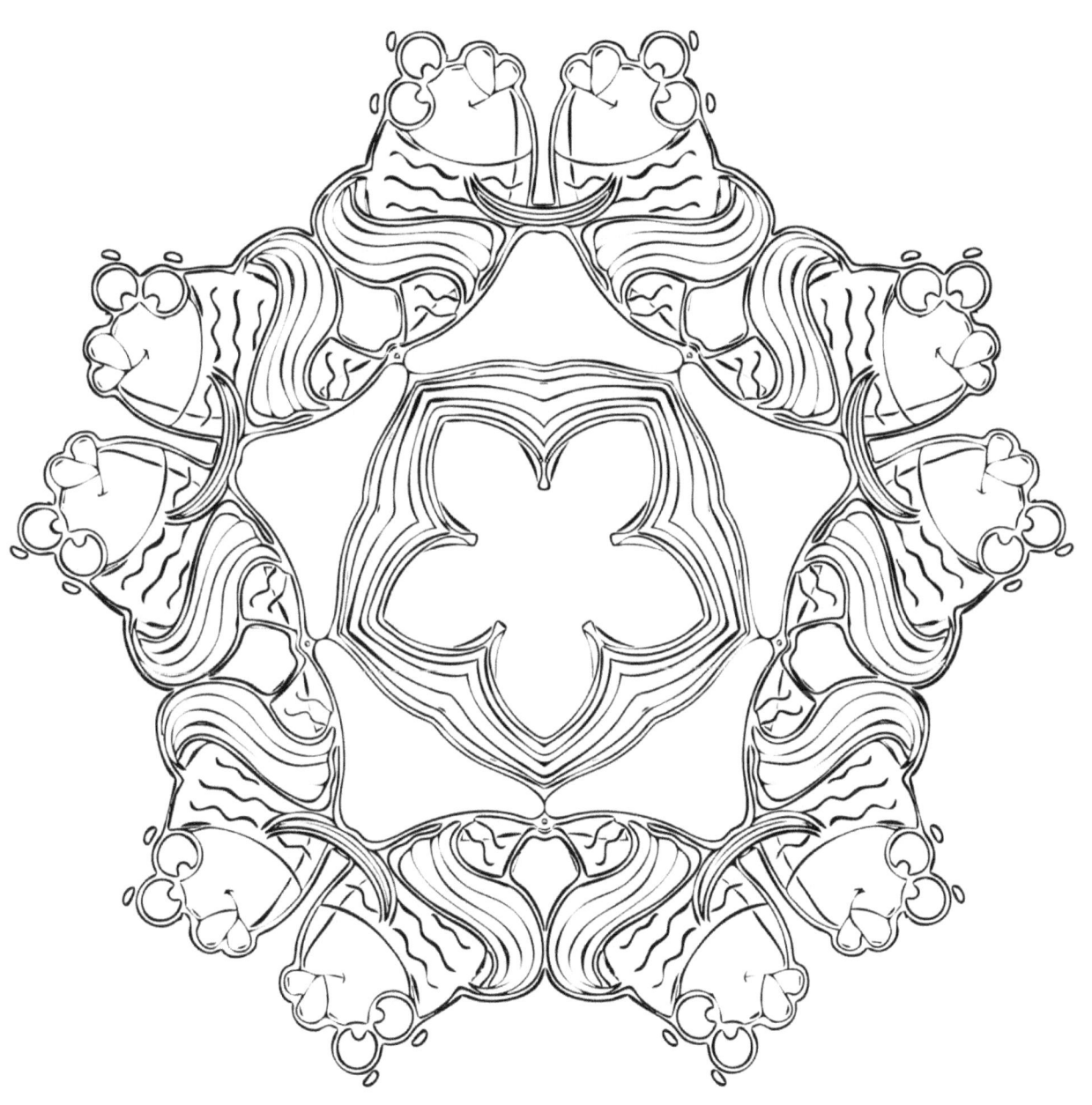

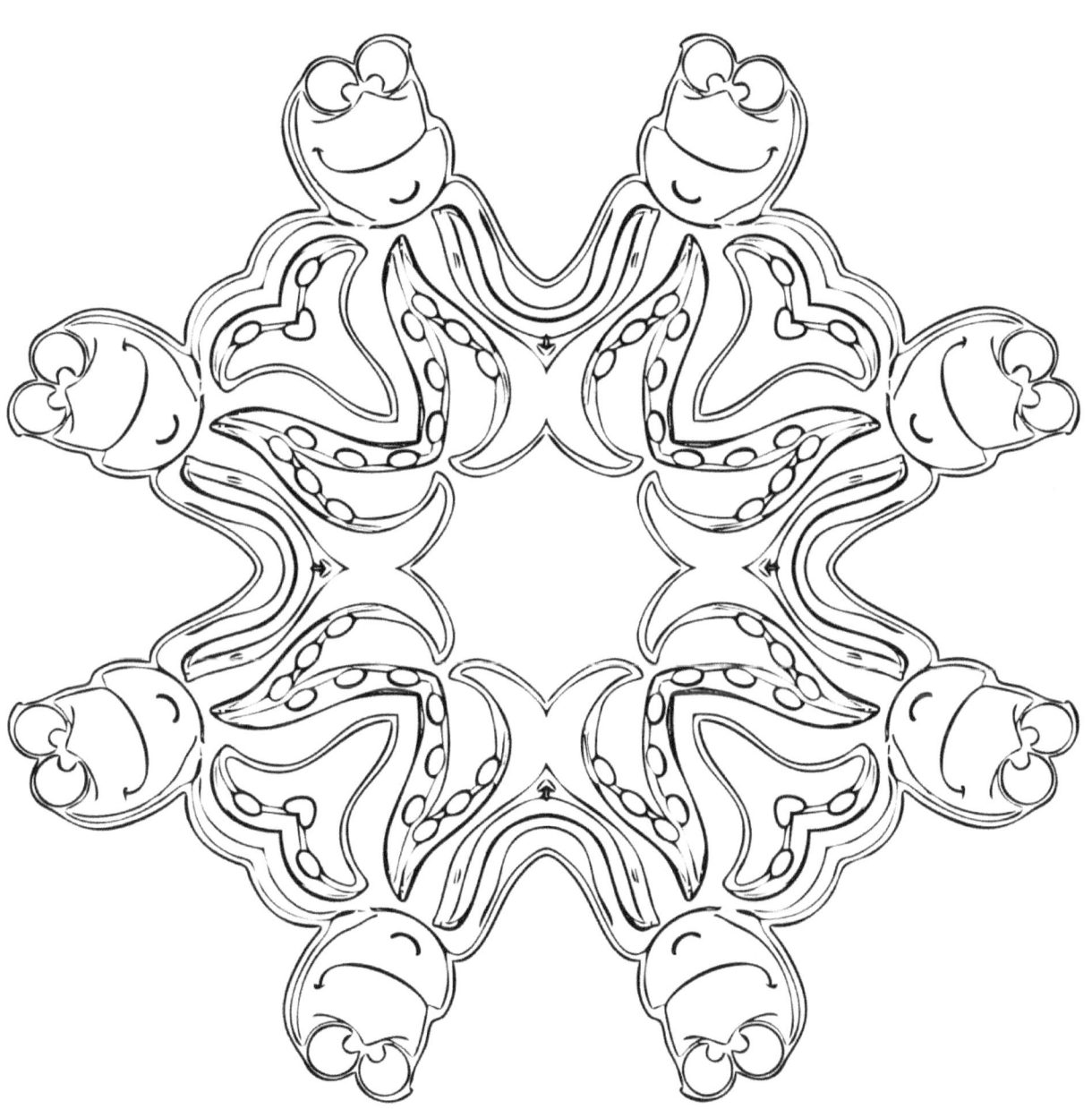

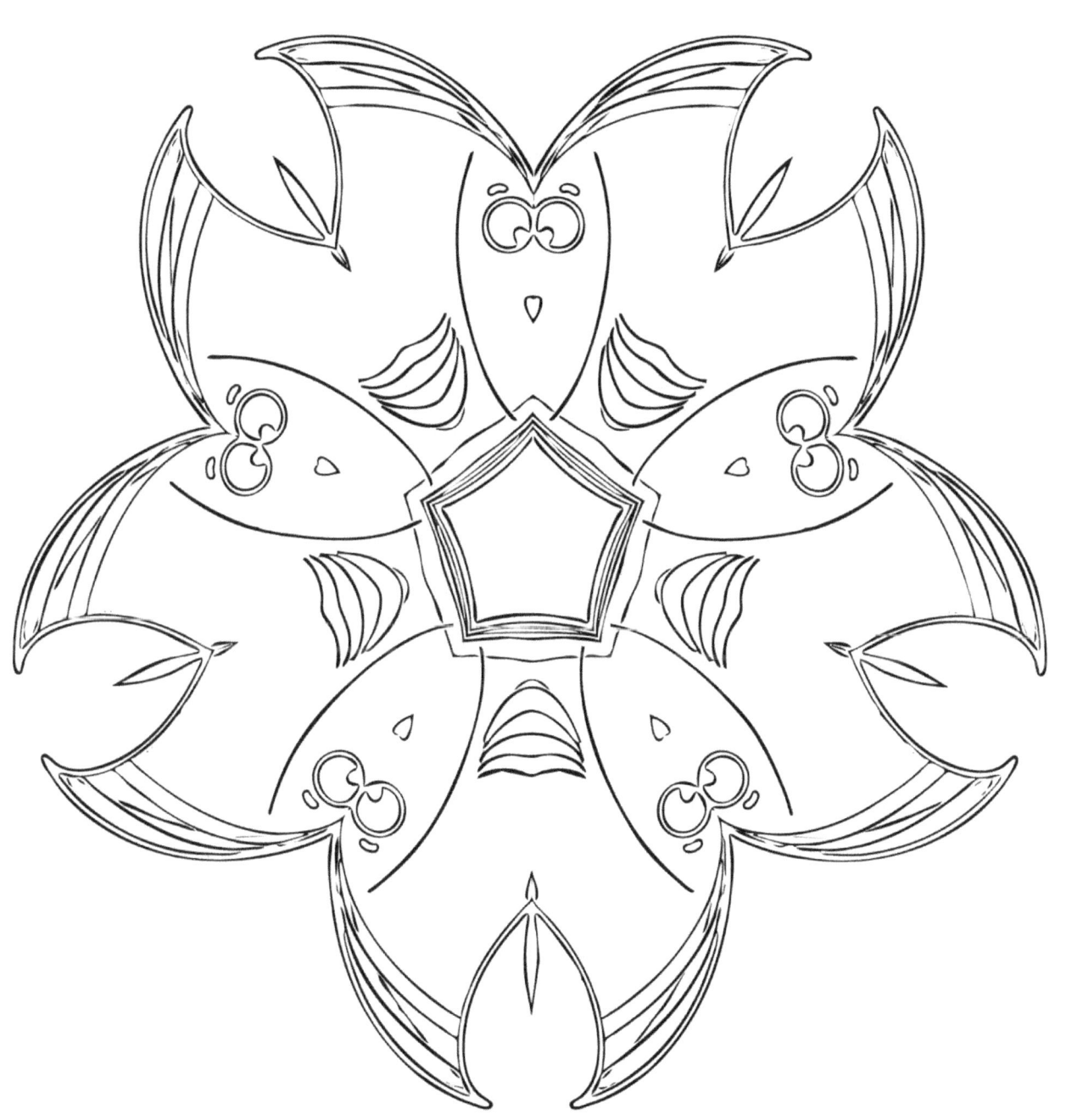

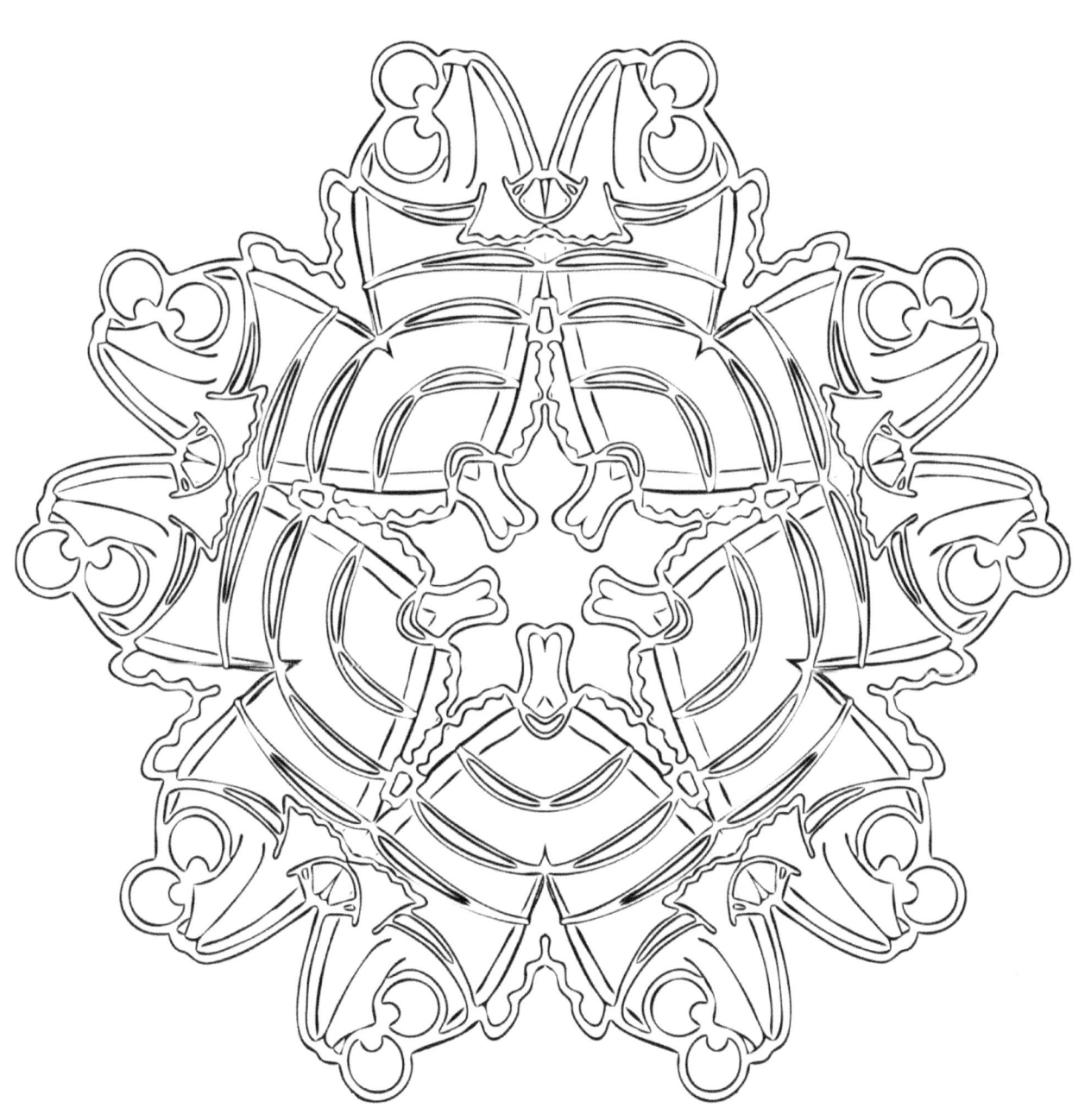

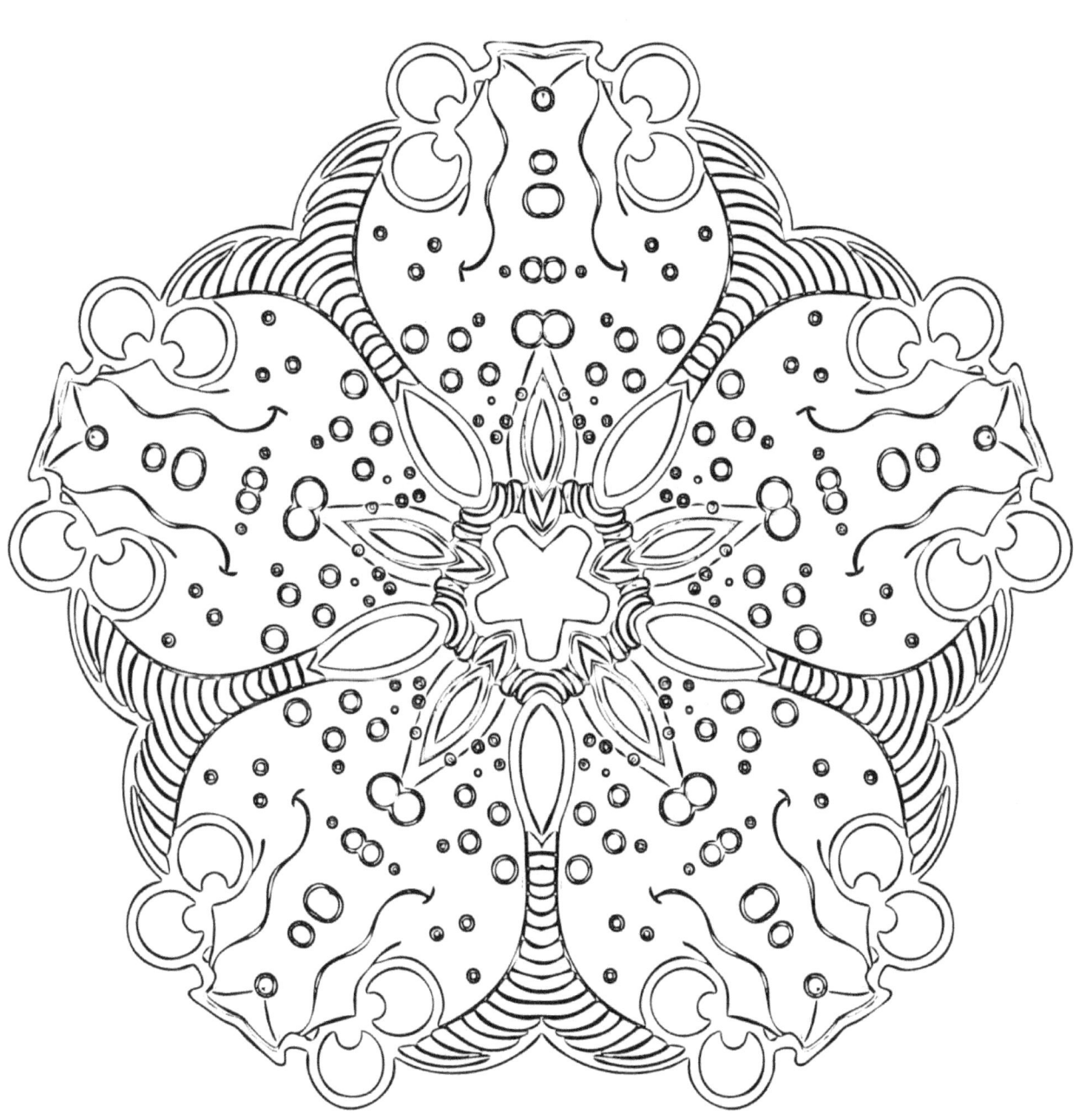

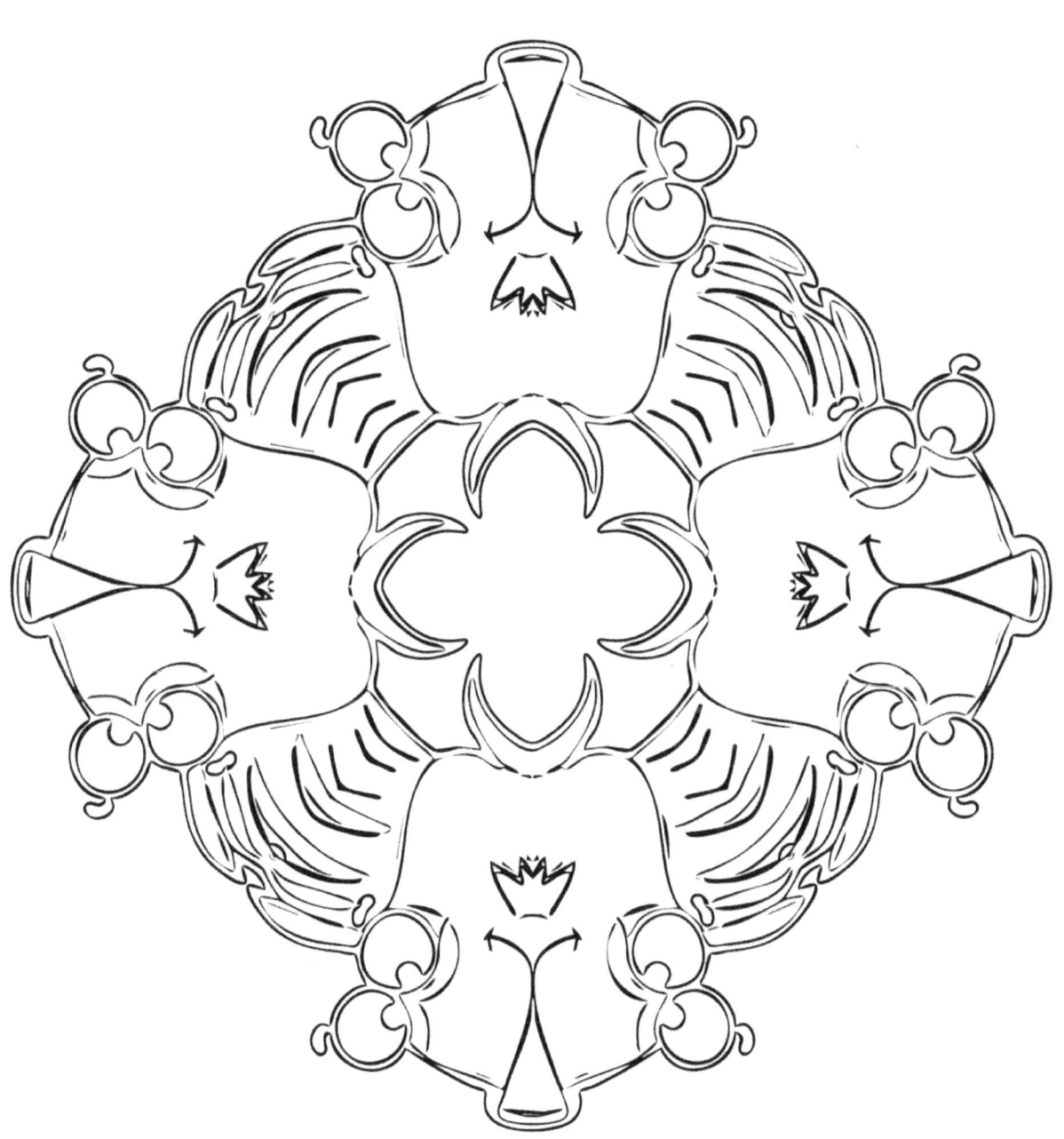

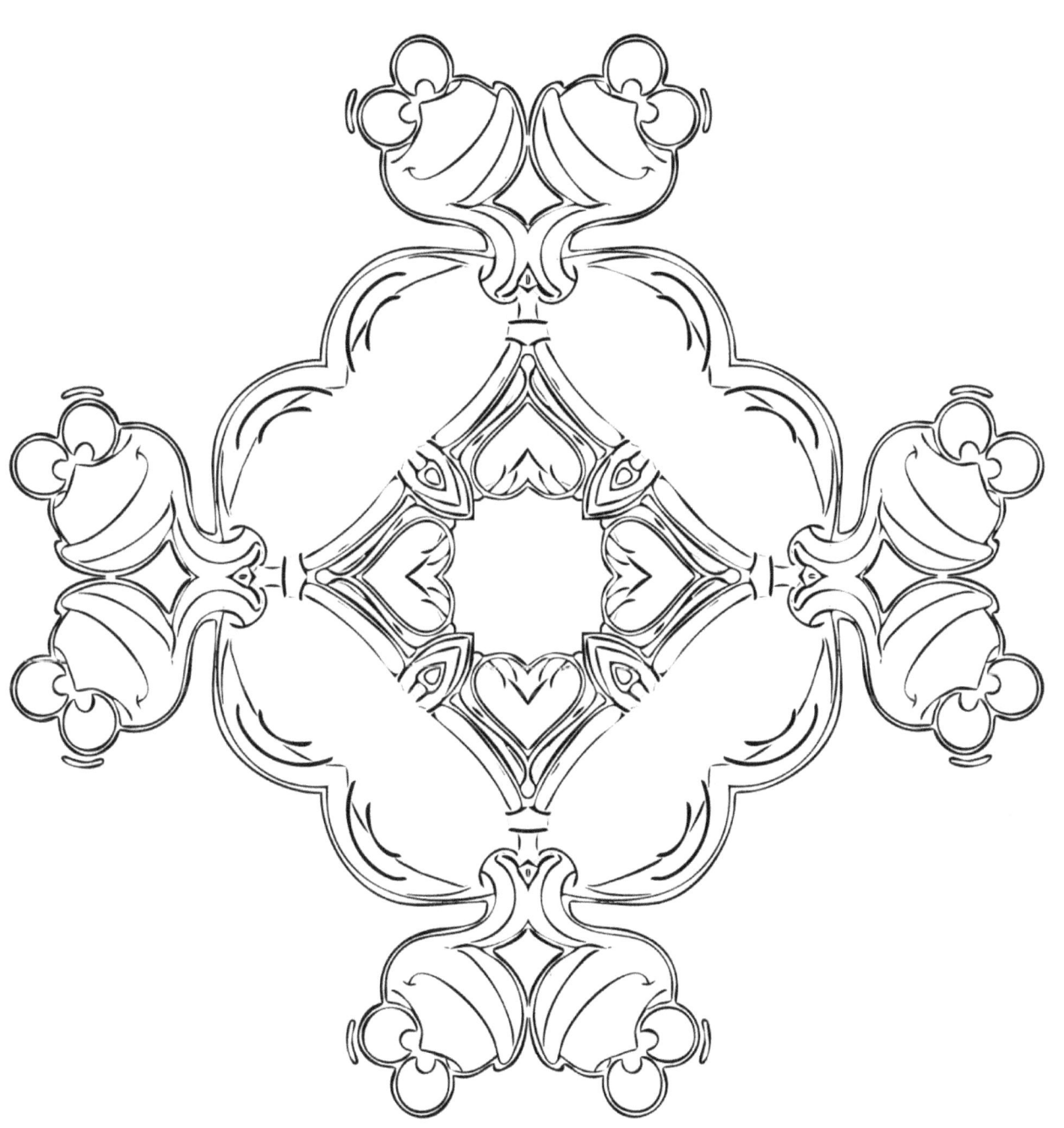

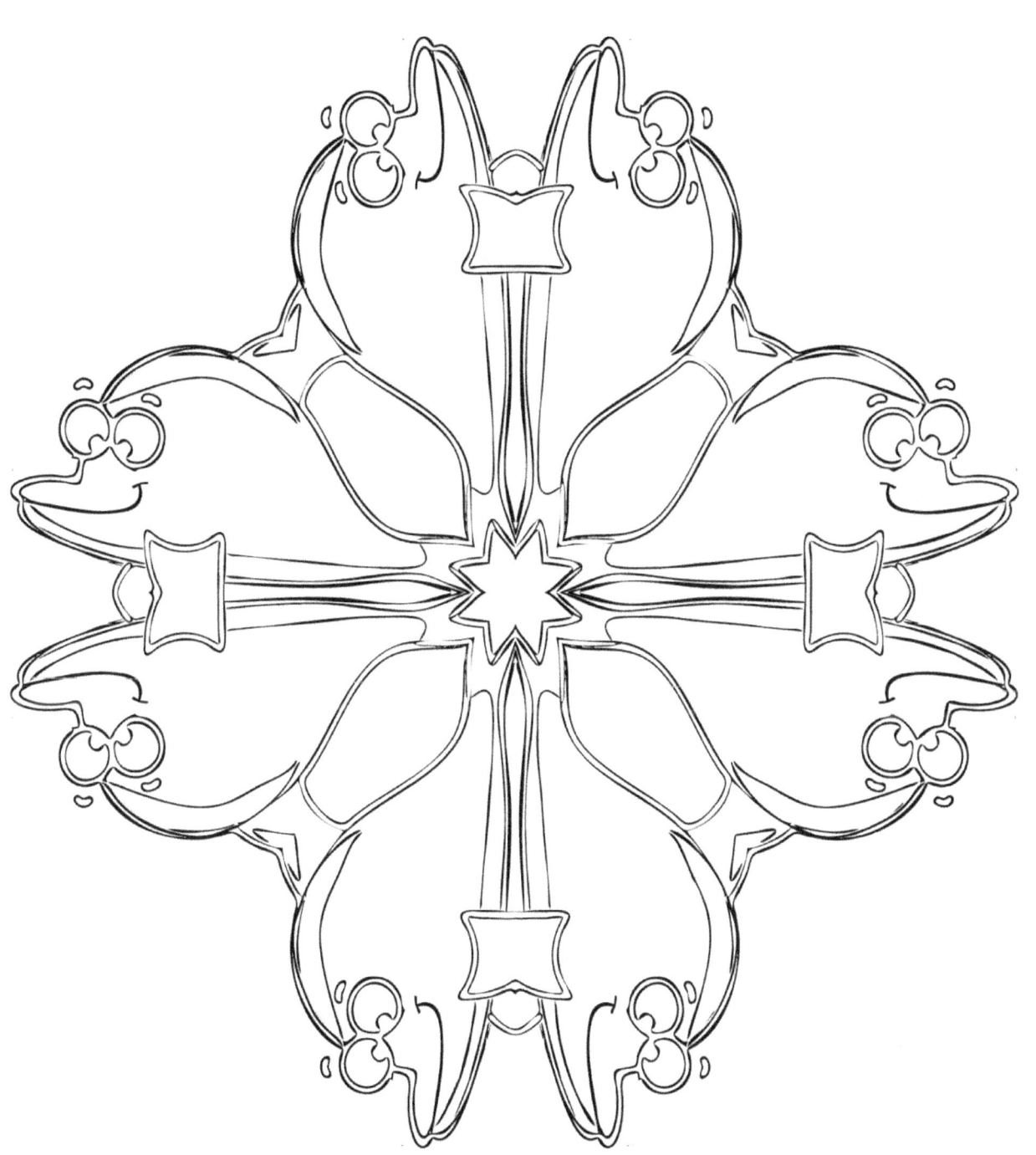

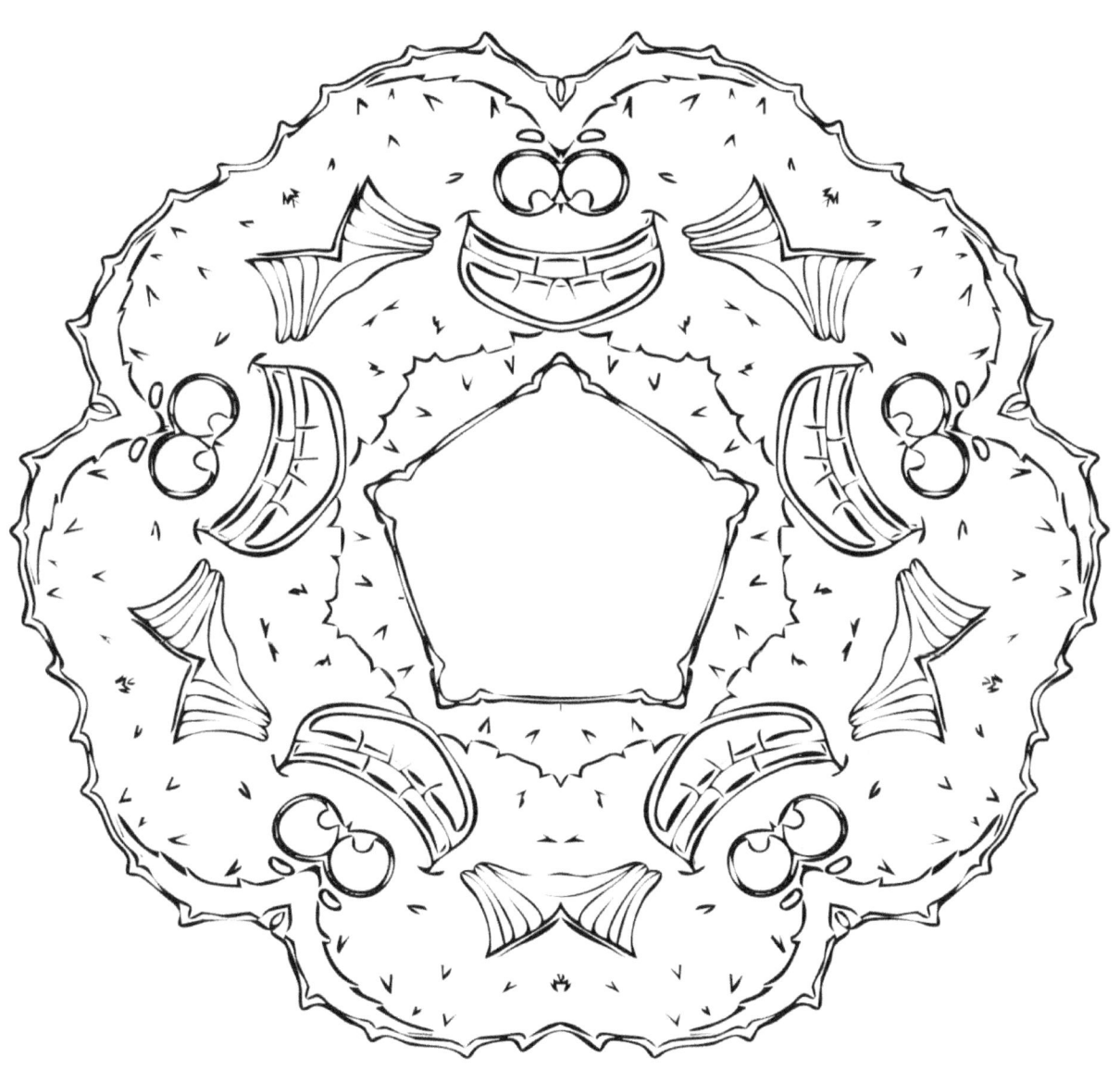

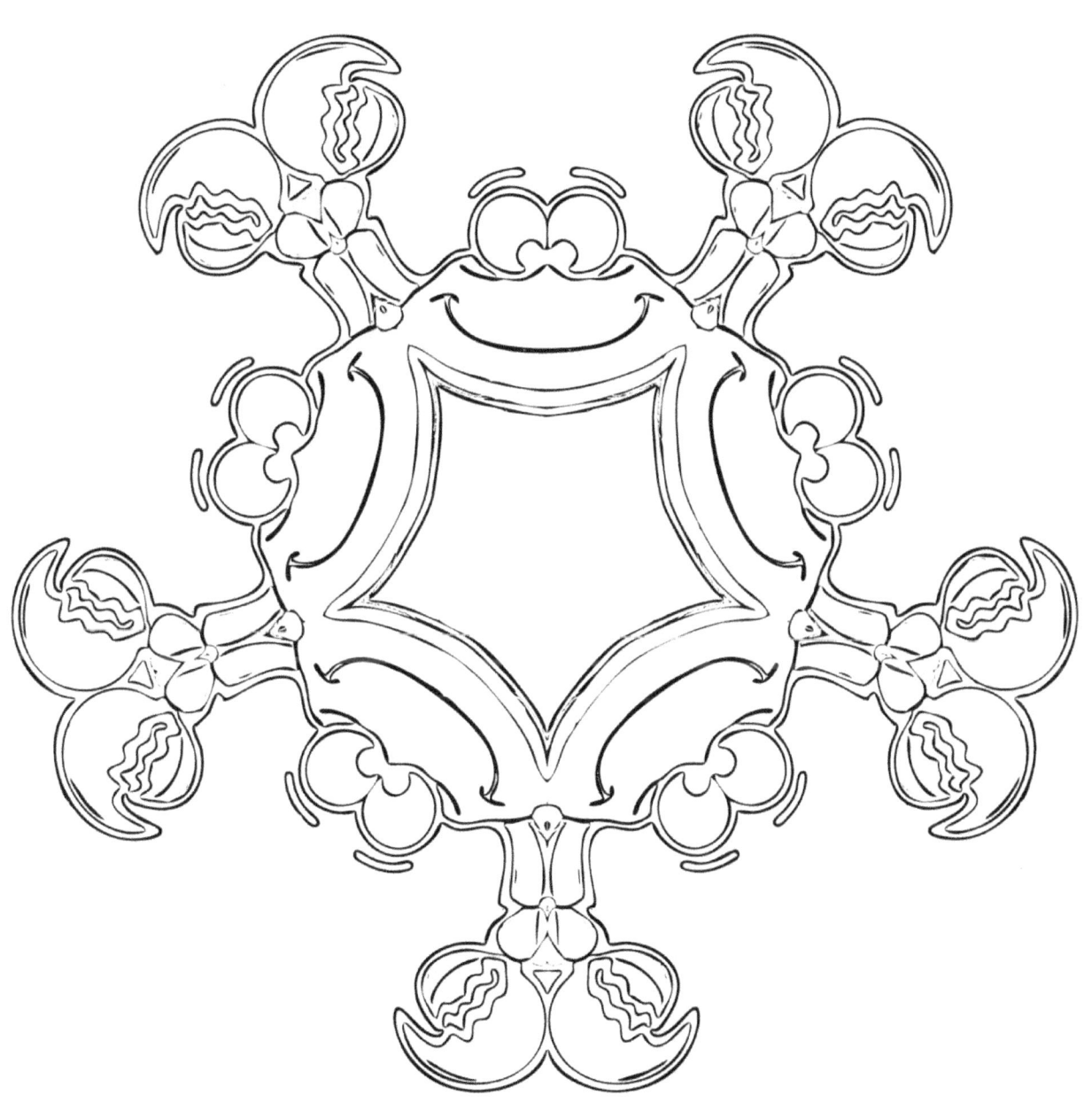

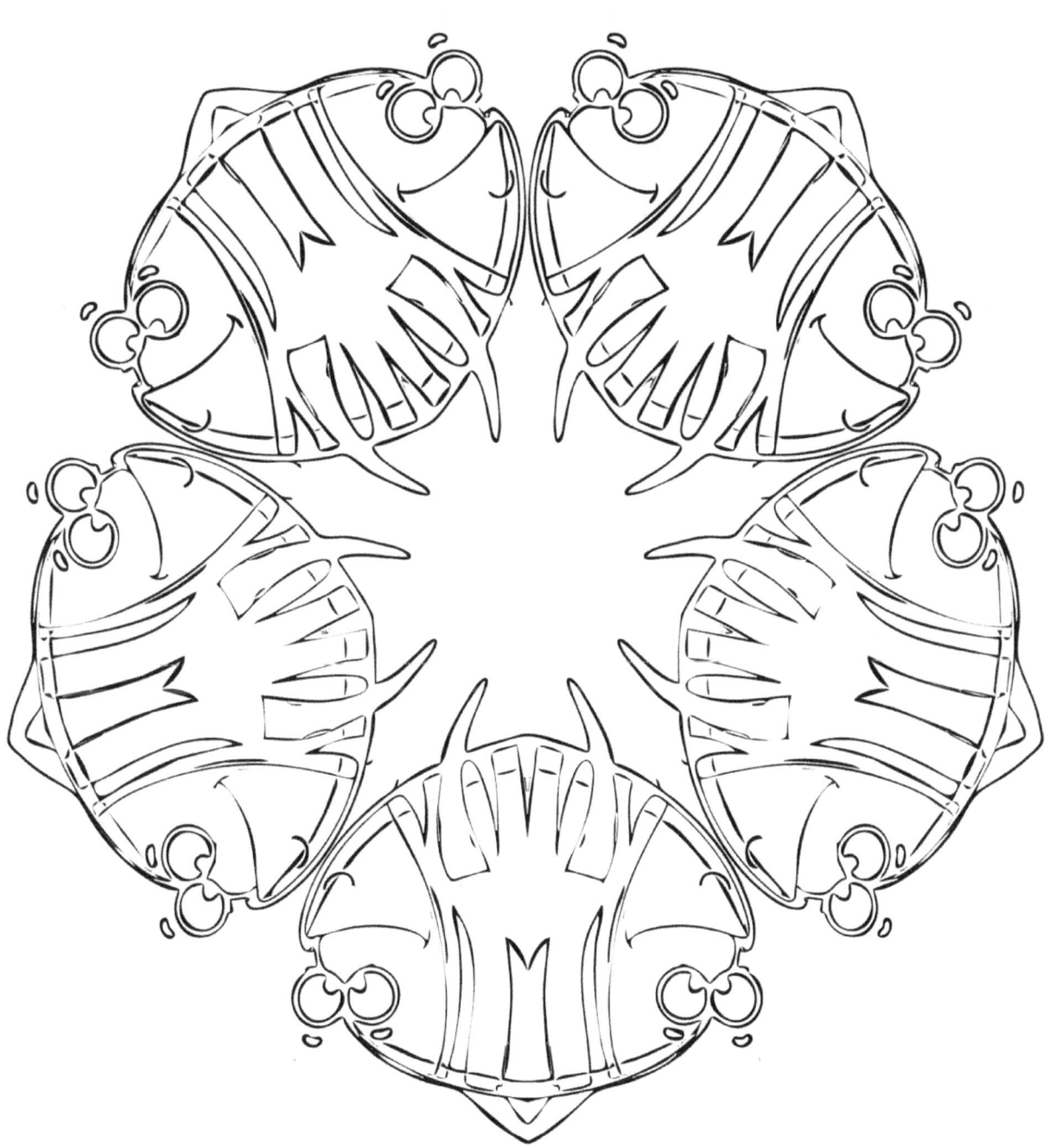

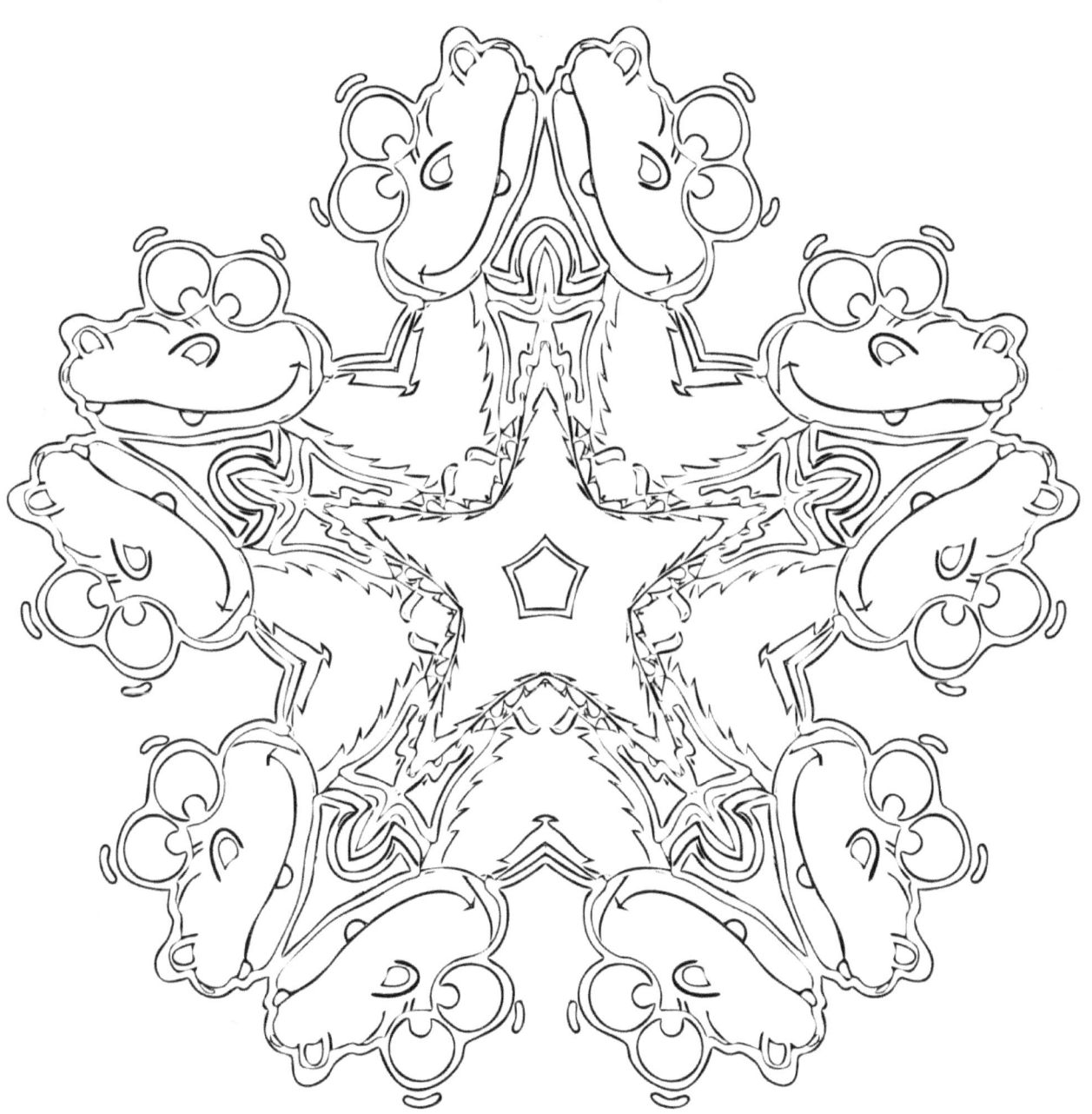

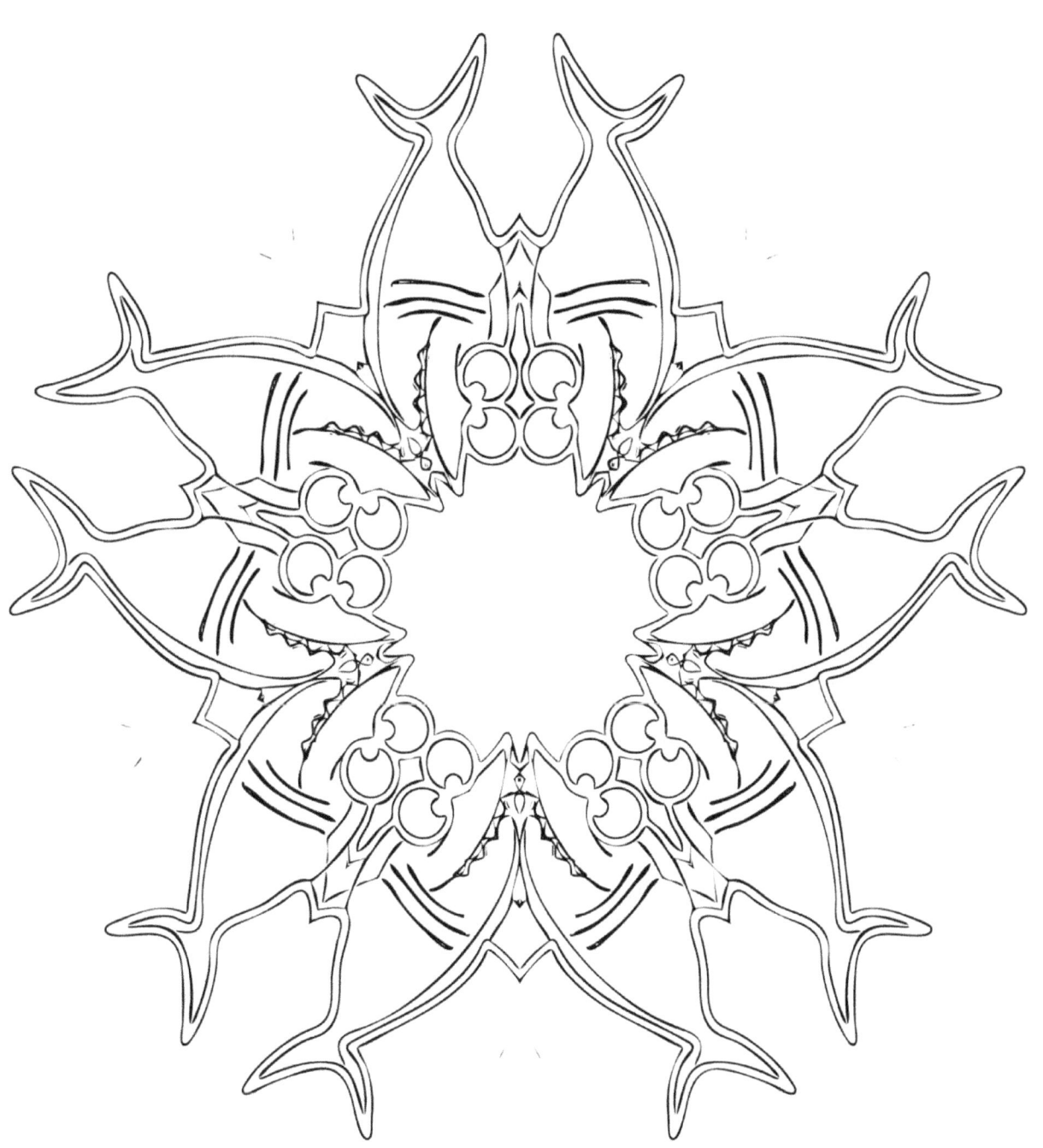

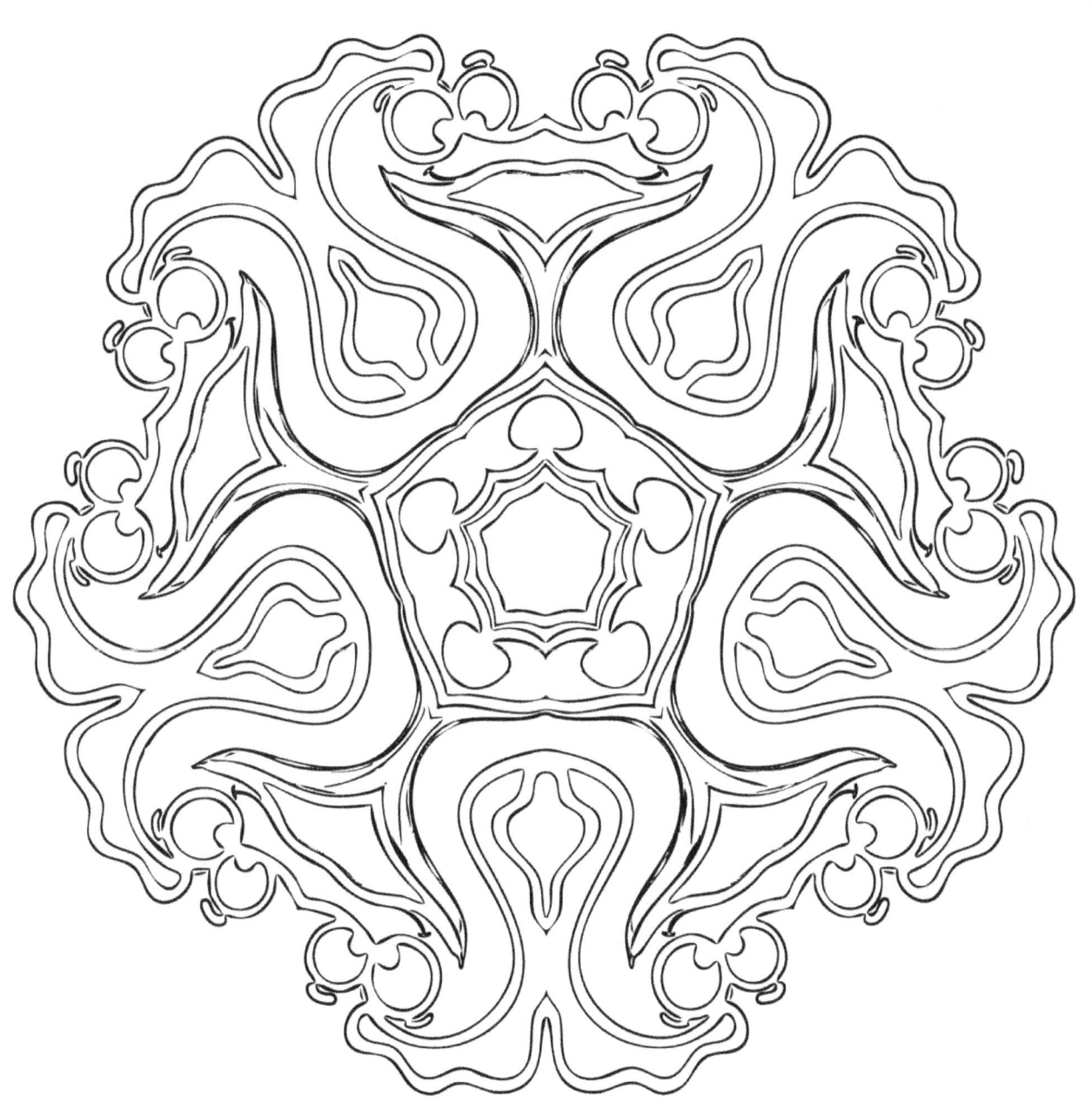

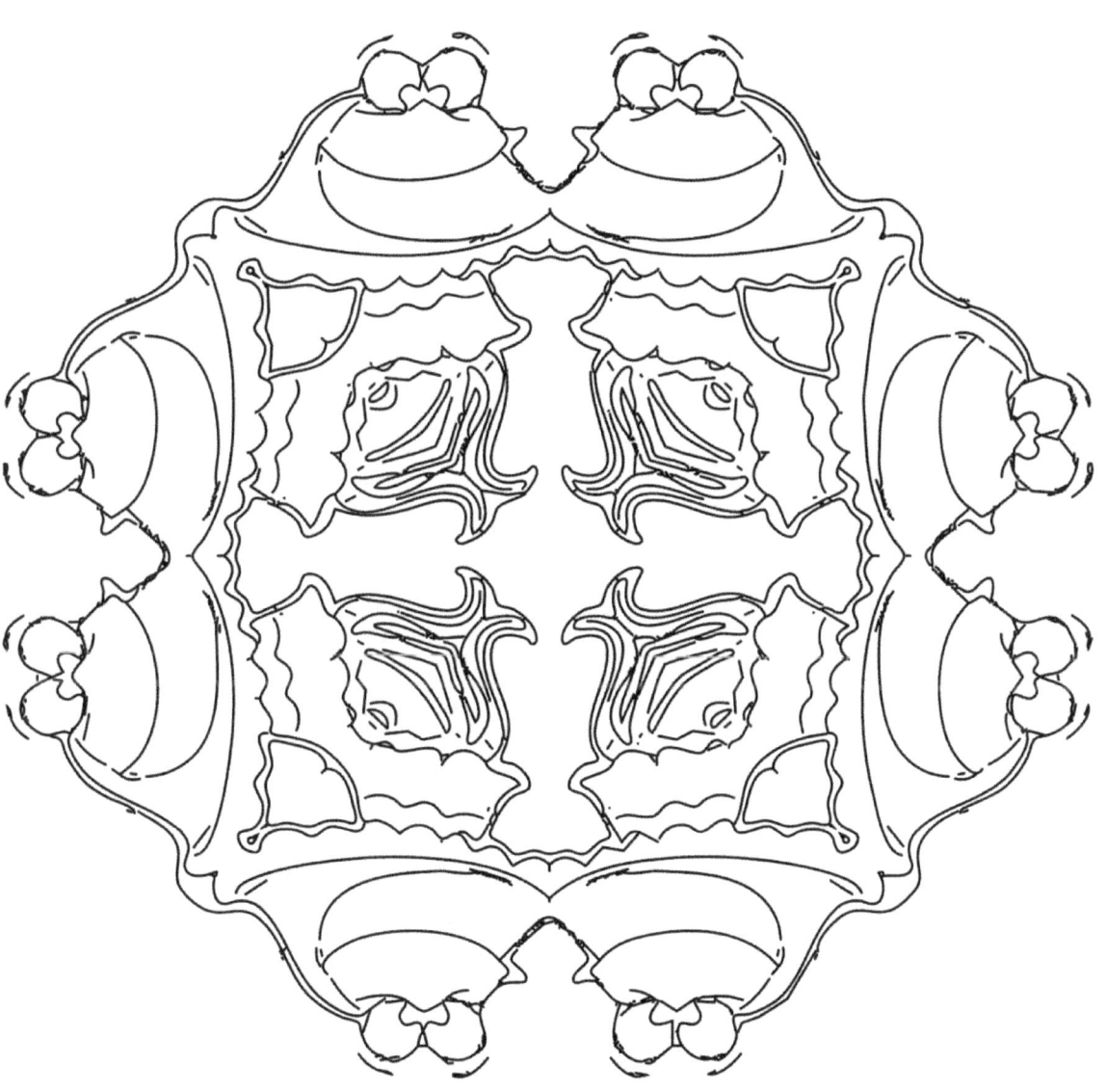

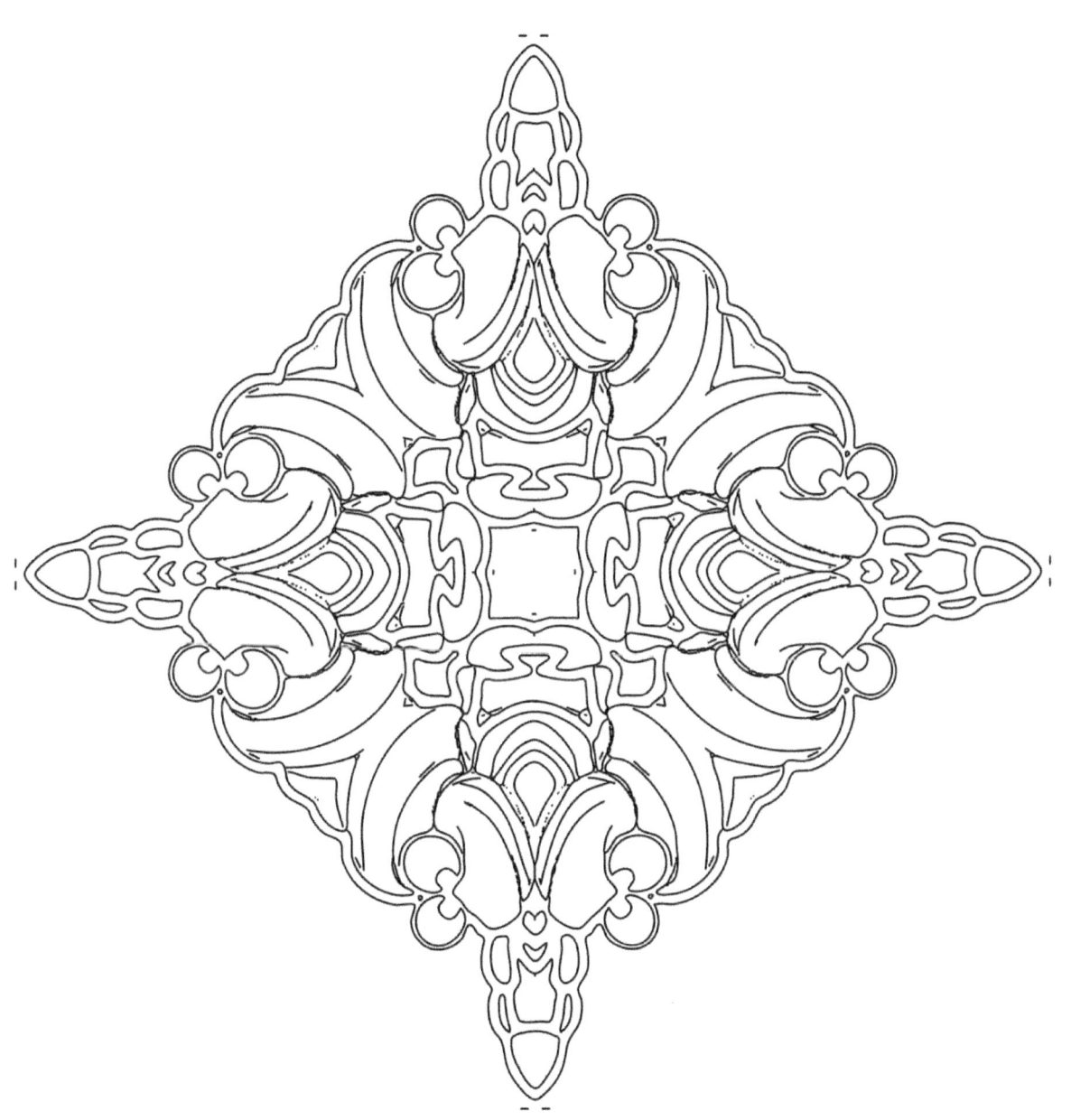

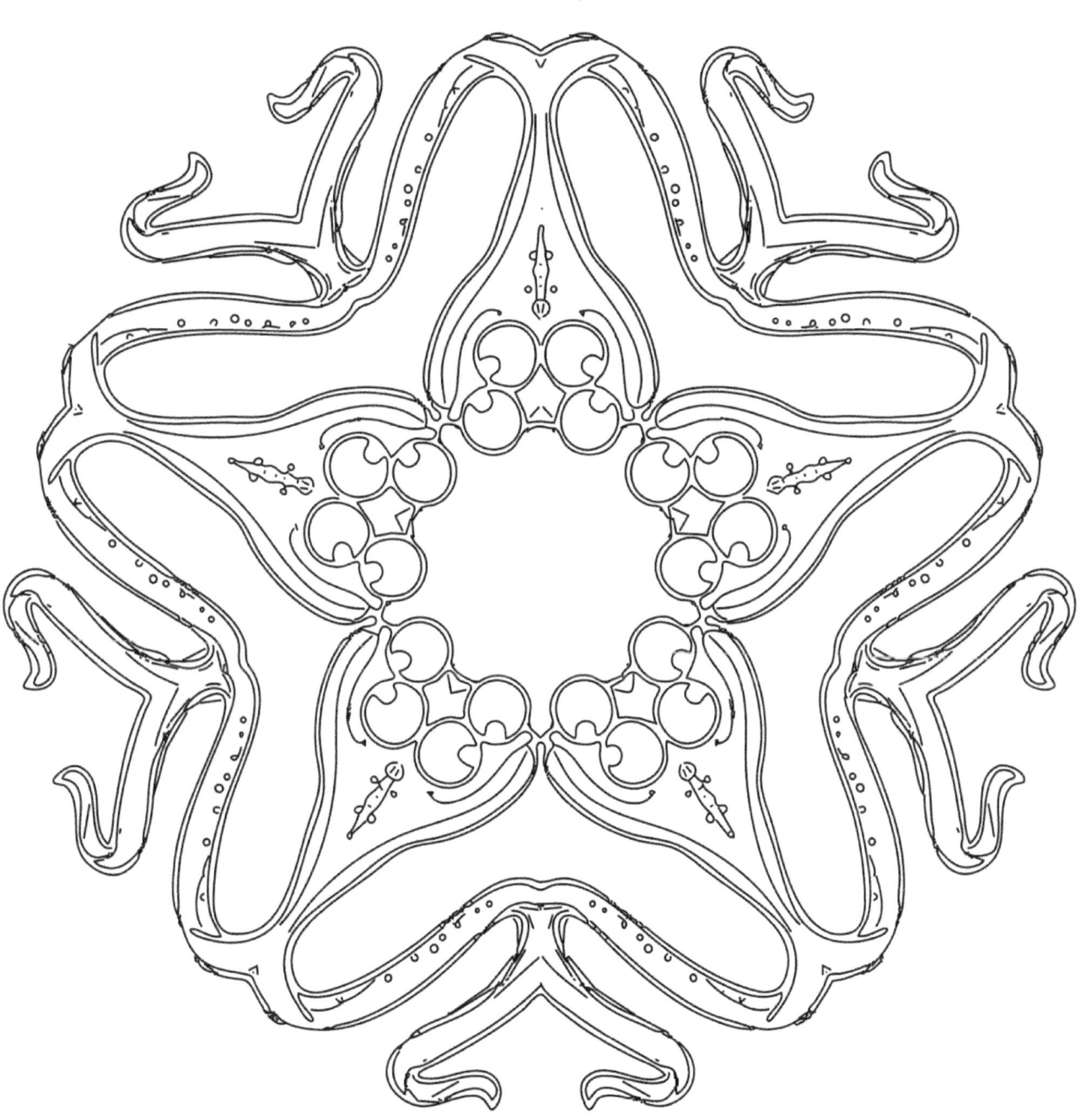

www.ingramcontent.com/pod-product-compliance
Lightning Source LLC
Chambersburg PA
CBHW080611180526
45168CB00007B/2864